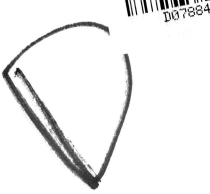

– Fast Tracks

– Indy Racing

A.T. McKenna

visit us at
www.abdopub.com

Published by Abdo & Daughters, 4940 Viking Drive, Suite 622, Edina, Minnesota 55435.
Copyright © 1998 by Abdo Consulting Group, Inc., Pentagon Tower, P.O. Box 36036, Minneapolis, Minnesota 55435 USA. International copyrights reserved in all countries. No part of this book may be reproduced in any form without written permission from the publisher.

Printed in the United States.

Cover and Interior Photo credits: Allsport USA, Duomo, SportsChrome, Superstock

Edited by Paul Joseph

Library of Congress Cataloging-in-Publication Data

McKenna, A. T.
   Indy racing / A. T. McKenna.
      p.   cm. -- (Fast tracks)
  Includes index.
  Summary: Examines Indy racing, a forum of auto racing based on the Indianapolis 500 race; discusses racing worldwide, building the cars, and what happens during the race.
   ISBN 1-56239-835-0
  1. Indianapolis Speedway Race--Juvenile literature. 2. Automobile racing--Indiana--Juvenile literature. I. Title II. Series: McKenna, A. T. Fast tracks
  GV1033.5.T55M34 1998
  796.72'09772'52--dc21

                                       97-46647
                                          CIP
                                          AC

−Contents

–The First Indy Race

Indy racing is one of the oldest and most prestigious forms of auto racing in the world. Indy race cars got their name from the Indianapolis 500, the most famous of all auto races. The Indianapolis 500 race is held each year on Memorial Day weekend in Indianapolis, Indiana.

On May 30, 1911, the very first Indianapolis 500 was held on a one mile oval track made of about 3.5 million bricks. The nickname for the track is "The Brickyard." In the early years, Indy race cars could only go about 75 miles per hour (120 kph). This meant that it could sometimes take over eight hours to complete the 500 mile (805km) race.

The first race started the tradition of opening the track for practice on the first of May. Forty-four racers showed up for practice for the first Indianapolis 500. Those who could average close to 75 miles per hour (120kph) were allowed to compete. The cars had two seats—one for the driver and one for the mechanic, who would watch for other cars and accidents during the race.

The first Indianapolis 500 was won by driver Ray Harroun. Over the years, asphalt has been placed over most portions of the bricks on the track for smoother racing. Now only a narrow strip of bricks remains at the start/finish line.

After the first Indianapolis 500, tracks were built all over the country to run Indy car races. Indy car tracks were also built outside of the United States. Tracks in other parts of the world include: Surfer's Paradise in Australia; Pacific Place in Vancouver, Canada; and Exhibition Place in Toronto, Canada.

Modern Indy cars can go 200 mph (322 kph) or faster.

<u>–On Track</u>

Indy race cars race on oval racetracks, road courses, and temporary tracks. Oval tracks are the most common type of Indy race car track. Although they are called ovals, these tracks actually look rectangular.

Cars race around the track in one direction—counter-clockwise. The tracks have very wide corners, which are on a slope or slant. These are called banked curves. Drivers can choose to go around the curves at a high, medium, or low level. Most of the crashes and bumping into the walls happens on the curves. The walls are made of solid concrete and have a fence on top to protect the spectators watching the race.

The long length of the track is called the straight-away. This is the area where the driver can really pick up speed. The start/finish line is located in the middle of the straight-away.

Road courses are another type of Indy race car track. These tracks have many different shapes and layouts. Many look like a maze with both curves and straight-aways, twists, and turns. Road courses are considered the most safe of the three types since they have run-off areas, places to pull over, and are not lined by concrete walls.

Temporary tracks are set up on closed sections of public roads, many times right in the middle of the city. An example of this type of track is the Long Beach Grand Prix in California. Races on temporary tracks attract lots of spectators, since fans don't have far to go to see the race. Sometimes people can watch the race right from their own backyard!

In recent times, two Indy race car series have been developed, each with their own set of races and rules. The two sanctioning organizations are the Indy Racing League (IRL) and Championship Auto Racing Teams (CART).

Concrete walls and high fences protect spectators at the Indianapolis 500.

A sanctioning organization is a group of officials who set the rules for racing, including how the cars are built. The sanctioning organization also decides the prize money for the winners and sets up a point system that determines which driver is the national champion at the end of the racing season.

−Building the Cars

An Indy race car looks similar to a Formula One car, but it is much bigger and heavier. One of the main components on an Indy car is the chassis, or frame, of the car. The chassis is made from a mold.

The mold is lined with several woven pieces of a material called carbon fiber. Carbon fiber is a very strong material that is dark in color and looks like Fiberglass. It is so strong, that it won't break unless it is hit very hard.

When it does break, it shatters into pieces. The mold and chassis are placed in a huge oven called an autoclave. The chassis is cooked at 380 degrees Fahrenheit for one to two hours until it is stiff and strong. The chassis must be very strong to protect the driver if there is a crash.

On an Indy race car, there are two very fragile pieces, the front wing and the rear wing. On an airplane, the wings help bring the plane up into the air. On a race car, the wings do the opposite. Indy race car wings are placed upside down, and when air passes over the wing, it pushes the car down so the car stays on the ground. The wings help the car grip the track better.

The wings are usually the last pieces to be attached to the car. The rear wing is much smaller than the front wing, and may seem a little flimsy. However, this carbon fiber piece can withstand downforce pressures of approximately 1,500 pounds (680kg). Downforce is the amount of air pressure pushing down on the wing.

Indy cars are built to be strong and safe for the driver.

–Under the Hood

Once the chassis is finished, the inside parts are put in place. These include the engine, fuel system, exhaust system, and cooling system.

The type of engine used in an Indy race car is called a V-8. These engines are rated at between 750 to 900 horsepower, which means the cars can race around the track at speeds of 200 miles per hour (322 kph) and higher. Engines in an Indy race car are placed behind the driver's seat. An Indy race car engine can cost over $200,000. The engine lasts only one race before it needs to be rebuilt. Rebuilding the engine costs an average of $50,000.

Indy race cars have large fuel tanks that are called fuel cells. The fuel cell is a puncture-resistant piece of rubber material over a bag. The rubber is rigid and thick enough that it can stand up on its own. This makes the fuel cell much harder to damage and prevents fuel from splattering out if there is a crash. The fuel cell must be placed on the chassis behind the driver's back. No fuel can be placed in front of the driver.

On a regular car, the exhaust pipes are found in the rear of the car, most of the time between the rear wheels. On an Indy race car, the exhaust pipes are on the rear side of the car, usually on

the left side. Many teams place the exhaust pipes on the side of the car so the pipes won't be blocked if the car turns and brushes against the wall of the track.

During the race, the engine gets very hot. Grill openings in the front and sides of the car help supply cool air to the engine area. The cooling system uses electric fans to cool down the radiator and brakes. The driver also gets quite hot inside the cockpit. Air vents and fans help keep the driver cool, too.

The pit crew makes adjustments to the car during a pit stop.

–The Tires are Turning

Racing tires and wheels are larger than those on a regular car. This helps to keep the car steady when going around a sharp curve or passing another car. The wheels have a lock device that helps keep the tires from flying off during the race.

Tire pressure, or how much air you put in the tire, can make a big difference in the performance of the car. The more pressure in the tire, the stiffer the tire becomes. A different amount of tire pressure is put in each of the four tires to help the car handle the best on the track.

Indy race cars use radial tires. Tires wear out very quickly during a race. Not all the tires are changed at once. The outside tires (right side of the car) are changed every two pit stops. The inside front left tire is changed every three pit stops. The inside left rear tire can usually stay on the car for the entire race, but it is changed with the inside front tire.

During a caution flag, the entire set of tires will be replaced since there is extra time. The old tires are replaced with new, warm tires, which are kept heated in an electric covering, much like a blanket. Warm tires grip the track better and allow the driver to go faster.

Sometimes a team can go through over a dozen sets of tires during the race weekend. A set of four race tires can cost about $1,200 each.

The weather plays a role in the type of tire placed on the car. If the track is a little wet and slippery, tires with lots of grooves are mounted on the Indy race cars. The extra grooves help the cars stick to the track. If the track is dry, smooth tires called slicks are used. The grooves would slow the car down on a dry track.

An Indy car can go through a dozen sets of tires in one weekend.

LAUREL
Spark Plugs

OIL

SPEED
LUBE

INTERNATI

EXIT

Indy cars look much like formula I cars but indy cars are bigger and heavier.

An indy race engine costs 200,000 dollars and must be rebuilt after each race at the cost of 50,000 dollars.

There are two forms of Indy racing: IRL and CART.

1 · 2 · 3 · 4

After the first Indy 500, racetracks were built all over the country and in Europe.

Ray Harroun won the first Indy 500.

DANLO TIRES

SAFE-T CLEANSE

BURGER HUT

1894- First official auto race from Paris to Rouen.

May 30, 1911- First running of the Indianapolis 500.

The average speed at the first Indy 500 was 75 mph (120kph).

The first Indy cars had two seats.

In the first Indy races, the mechanics rode in the cars with the drivers.

–From the Cockpit

The cockpit, or driver's area, of an Indy race car doesn't look anything like a regular car. Most of the changes are made for the safety and protection of the driver. A roll bar that is part of the chassis is required. The roll bar is an upside down "U" shaped bar that is very strong and is padded with foam to protect the driver's head. If a car crashes and flips over during a race, the weight of the car will be on the roll bar, not the driver.

Each car is fitted with a Halon fire extinguishing system. If there is a fire in the cockpit, the fire extinguisher will start spraying automatically. The driver doesn't even need to push a button!

The dash board holds a great deal of information. All the important gauges like the speedometer, fuel gauge, and engine information are now computerized. The numbers are digital on a screen on the dashboard. When drivers are traveling at speeds over 200 miles per hour (322 kph), they don't have time to look down and find the needle on the gauge. Numbers on a screen make it easy to see how much fuel is left or how fast the car is going.

The steering wheel on an Indy race car is a "quick-release" steering wheel, which means it comes off fast, if needed. By pulling a pin and tugging a little, the steering wheel will come off

An Indy car cockpit is nothing like a regular car.

and make extra space so the driver can easily get out of the car. The steering wheel on an Indy race car has a button to operate a radio. The driver presses the button to speak to the crew chief during the race.

The driver has a special bucket-style seat which fits the driver's body snugly. This type of seat is more comfortable when the car is traveling at high speeds. The seat has padding to protect the ribs and a special padded headrest. The headrest will help prevent injuries to the neck and head in case of an accident. A seat belt, called a safety harness, makes sure the driver won't be moved out of place during the race.

In order to race competitively, a racer must be able to slow down to avoid accidents and eventually stop when the race is over. The driver needs to rely on the brakes when going around a turn or when pulling over for a tire change. The brakes in an Indy race car are called disc brakes and are made of steel. They are much stronger than brakes in a regular car, and they allow the driver to stop very quickly.

–*Colored Cars and Safety*

Now that the car is assembled, it's time for a coat of paint. Indy race cars are brightly painted, with the names and labels of the companies who help to pay for the car. These companies are called sponsors. The primary sponsor of the race team determines the main colors the car is painted.

Rules specify where the car number should be displayed on the car and the minimum size the number must be. The car number is painted on the

The sponsor determines the color of the car.

front, on each side of the car, and to the back of the car on the rear wing. It must be placed so it can be seen from all angles, even from the official's tower above the track.

Every bit of clothing the driver wears must be made of special safety materials. Drivers must wear driving suits that are fireproof.

They are usually made of a material called Nomex. The driver wears a balaclava under the helmet. This looks like a ski mask and is made of fireproof material. Socks, gloves, shoes, even underwear must be fireproof. This is to protect the driver in the case of an engine fire while driving or during a crash.

A high-quality helmet is one of the most important pieces of the driver's gear. The helmet could save a driver's life during a crash. Many times the helmet is made of carbon fiber, just like the chassis. The helmet is fitted with a life

support system. This helps give the driver oxygen if there is a crash. There are vents in the helmet to keep the driver cool.

Opposite page: A driver must wear safety gear including a helmet and fireproof clothing.

–The Race Team

At one time there was only a driver and a mechanic. Today, there is an entire race team. The crew chief is the head of the race team and is in charge of the pit crew. The crew chief also works with the engine builder to help gain a competitive edge. The pit crew is a team of mechanics who prepare the car for the race and work on the car during the race.

Each member of the pit crew has a job. There are tire changers, fuelers, engineers to work on the engine, a score keeper to log the laps, and even a crew member to give the driver some water and wipe off the goggles. All of these pit crew members must work well together to keep the driver out on the track.

Qualifying day for an Indy race usually takes place a couple days before the race. During this time, the driver and his race team work closely together to get the best spot in the line-up of cars for race day.

With Indy race cars there are two types of qualifying. If racing on an oval, the driver is allowed two fast laps around the track. The fastest lap will determine if the racer is in the starting lineup. There is only one racer on the track at a time.

If the race is a road course, each driver is given two sessions on the course to record the fastest lap. The driver is not the only

one on the course. Other drivers who are trying to qualify are driving on the course as well. This makes road course qualifying difficult.

Before attempting to qualify, each driver is given two warm-up laps. The pit crew must signal with a green flag that a qualifying attempt is being made. The driver with the fastest qualifying time is called the pole sitter. This driver will start the race in the front row. Those who do not qualify well or crash during qualifying end up at the very end of the line. There are a certain amount of spots available for any race. Not every driver will get a spot in the line-up.

A race team must work together with precision.

−Practice Day and Flags

The day after qualifying day is called practice day. This day is spent setting up the car and practicing for the race the following day. This day is very critical to drivers. It is the last chance the driver will have to go around the track until the actual race. It is also the last chance the race team will have to prepare the car before the race. This includes working on the engine, brakes, and handling of the car.

Two cars are taken to the track for a race weekend. One is the primary car driven, and the other is a backup. The backup car is used in case the primary car gets damaged during practice or qualifying.

Race officials use different colored flags to communicate with the drivers on the race track. There are many flags used, each with a different meaning. A green flag is used to signal the start of the race. When a driver sees the green flag waving, it means "GO." The green flag is also used to restart the race.

A yellow flag tells the drivers to be careful, stop passing, slow down, and that there is a dangerous situation ahead. A red flag means the race is being stopped. Drivers are usually instructed to go into the pits or line up in a certain area when there is a red flag waving.

A white flag with a red diagonal stripe tells the drivers that an emergency or service vehicle is on the track. Drivers should slow down and be careful. A black flag pointed at a certain driver's car means the driver must go to the pits immediately. This flag means the car may not be safe to drive, or the driver is racing dangerously.

A white flag means that the leader of the race has started the last lap of the race. Only one lap to go! Probably the flag most drivers want to see as they pass the start/finish line is the checkered flag. When the winning car crosses the finish line, this flag is waved.

A race crew congratulates a driver after a qualifying run.

-Race Day

On race day, the race teams arrive early and get all the equipment set up in the pits. Last minute repairs are made and all the parts of the car are checked and re-checked to make sure the car is ready to race. The car is then pushed out to the starting grid, the area on the track where the race will start.

The order in which the cars line up was decided during qualifying, two days before. Marks on the starting grid show where the cars are to be placed. The pole sitter is placed in the front row in the inside lane. Usually the cars on the starting grid are covered with nylon covers to keep the interior cool.

After the cars are on the starting grid, they will not be started until the race begins. The cars must stay in their places until the green flag waves and the start/finish line is crossed.

During the race drivers make pit stops. A pit stop is when the driver comes off the track during the race to have repairs made to the car. The driver goes down pit road to the spot where the pit crew is waiting. The pit crew must work together as a team to help get the driver back on the track as soon as possible. Every second a driver spends in the pits, can cost the driver laps on the track. Only six crew members are allowed to work on the car in the pit area during the race.

The car has air jacks built underneath that raise the car up so the crew member can change the tires. During a pit stop, tires are changed, fuel is added, the driver's goggles are cleaned, and the driver is given a drink, all in less than 20 seconds!

Adding fuel takes up the most amount of time during a pit stop. Up to 40 gallons of fuel are added with two hoses. One hose pours the fuel into the car, and the other hose catches any

The Miami Grand Prix in 1995

spills and puts the spilled fuel back into the tank.

The pit crew practices pit stops many times before the actual race so that they can be as fast as possible. If one member of the team fails to do the job right, or bumps into another team member during a pit stop, it can cost the driver the race. It's a lot of pressure being on a pit crew. Pit stops can win or lose the race.

-Victory Lane

The race is officially over when the first car crosses the finish line with the checkered flag. When the winner and the second and third place finishers cross the finish line, the drivers are said to be in Victory Lane. This is where three drivers are presented with trophies and prize money.

The race result is only official 30 minutes after the race has ended. This gives the officials time to make sure all the records are correct. Now it's time to celebrate the victory and pack up the race car and start preparing to win the next race!

Becoming a professional Indy race car driver takes practice and years of experience. Most famous Indy race car drivers started out racing at their local tracks. Some of the cars start out in kart racers, midget cars, sprint cars, and silver crown cars. These are all circle track forms of racing, meaning the cars race on oval tracks.

Opposite page:The dream of every race car driver is to drive down victory lane.

–*Glossary*

Autoclave - A huge oven used to make the carbon fiber chassis of an Indy race car.

Championship Auto Racing Teams (CART) - A sanctioning body for Indy race cars.

Chassis - The frame of the car. The chassis is made of woven carbon fiber.

Checkered Flag - When the winning car crosses the finish line, this flag is waved, signaling the race is over.

Crew chief - The crew chief is in charge of organizing the pit crew, overseeing the preparation of the car and working with the engine builder.

Fuel cell - A large fuel tank used on Indy race cars. The fuel cell is a puncture-resistant piece of rubber material over a bag.

Indianapolis 500 - The most famous of all auto races. The Indianapolis 500 race is held each year on Memorial Day weekend in Indianapolis, Indiana.

Indy Racing League (IRL) - A sanctioning body for Indy race cars. This organization runs the Indianapolis 500 as well as other races.

Methanol - Indy race cars use methanol fuel (a type of alcohol) instead of gasoline. Methanol is made of oxygen, hydrogen, and carbon.

Pit crew - Members of the race team who help change tires and refuel during the race.

Pit stop - When the driver needs new tires or more fuel, the driver comes off the track during the race and makes a pit stop.

Pole sitter - The driver who had the fastest time during qualifying. This driver starts right in front at the race.

Qualifying - During qualifying, drivers compete for the fastest qualifying speed, which will determine their spot in the lineup of the race.

Quick-release - Equipment that is easy to remove quickly. The steering wheel in an Indy race car is quick-release.

Roll bar - A required part of the chassis. The roll bar is an upside down "U" shaped bar that is very strong and is padded with foam to protect the driver's head.

Safety harness - The special seat belt that keeps the driver from moving around while racing.

Slicks - Smooth tires used on Indy race cars.

Spectators - People who come to watch the race.

Sponsors - Companies who help pay for the car.

Starting grid - The area on the track where the cars line up to begin the race.

−*Internet Sites*

Formula 1 Links Heaven
http://ireland.iol.ie/~roym/
This site includes official sites, latest news, drivers, teams, computer games, circuits, mailing lists. This site has sound and video, very colorful and interactive.

Drag Racing on the net
http://www.lm.com/~hemi/
This is a cool and interactive sight with sound and fun photos.

Indyphoto.com
http://www.indyphoto.com/index.htm
This award winning site has excellent photographs of Indy Cars and it is updated on a regular basis.

MotorSports Image Online
http://www.msimage.com/index2.htm
This site gives you standings, results, schedules, teams, news, and a photo gallery.

Extreme Off-Road Racing
http://www.calpoly.edu/~jcallan/
This site has pre-runners, chat rooms, videos, racing pictures, wrecks, links, and much more extreme off-road racing stuff.

These sites are subject to change. Go to your favorite search engine and type in car racing for more sites.

Pass It On

Racing Enthusiasts: educate readers around the country by passing on information you've learned about car racing. Share your little-known facts and interesting stories. Tell others what your favorite kind of car is or who your favorite racer is. We want to hear from you!

To get posted on the ABDO & Daughters website E-mail us at "Sports@abdopub.com"

Visit the ABDO & Daughter website at www.abdopub.com

–Index